CONTROL THE CHAOS

Become a Star at Work Without Becoming a Stranger at Home

NATIONAL INSTITUTE OF
BUSINESS MANAGEMENT

Special Report PCCBS

Author: Liza Wheeler
Marketing Director: Linda Smith
Publisher: Phillip Ash

ISBN: 1-880024-14-4

"This publication is designed to provide accurate and authoritative information in regard to the subject matter covered. It is sold with the understanding that the publisher is not engaged in rendering legal, accounting or other professional service. If legal advice or other expert assistance is required, the services of a competent professional person should be sought."—*From a Declaration of Principles jointly adopted by a committee of the American Bar Association and a committee of publishers and associations.*

CONTENTS

INTRODUCTION   1

PRODUCTIVITY   3

Cultivate Creativity in a Changing Workplace   3

The Do's and Don'ts of Tighter Budgets   3

Make the Most of Fewer Resources   4

Improve Your Writing—Instantly   5

Make Work Interruptions Work for You   6

Get Technologically Savvy, *Now*   7

The Downside of E-mail   8

Strike the Right Balance Between Your Work/Personal Life   9

More Help in Emergencies   10

Keep Your Friendships Fresh and Rewarding   11

Fitting It All in   11

ORGANIZATION   13

Fine-Tune Your Skills to Improve Efficiency   13

Prioritize Like a Pro   13

What If *Everything* Is a Priority?   14

Are You Organized? A Short Quiz   15

File Review: Retrieve Anything—Instantly   16

Is E-mail Filing Different From Paper Filing?   18

5 Secrets to Better Organization   18

Learn to Purge Your Paper Files   19

Keep Track of the Deadlines and the Details   20

Managing a Poor Time Manager   20

OFFICE POLITICS   23

The Importance of Knowing the Game   23

10 Secrets to Mastering Office Politics   23

Ensure Your Success   25

Working Effectively for Multiple Bosses   26

How Do You Tell Your Boss He's Wrong?   26

Learn to Say 'No'—and Delight Your Boss   27

Have Difficult Bosses Eating Out of the Palm of Your Hand   28

Be *Politely* Disagreeable   28

She's Blaming You for Her Mistake ... Again   29

Become Your Boss's Greatest Asset   30

RECOGNITION   33

Get Rewarded for a Job Well Done   33

5 Ways to Earn Respect, Not Blame   34

Ask for a Raise in This Penny-Pinching Era? You Betcha!   35

I. INTRODUCTION

The phone won't stop ringing, six colleagues have interrupted you, your boss has missed two meetings, the printer is jammed again—*and it's not even 10 a.m.* Sound familiar? The life of today's administrative professional is no picnic, and it's only going to get busier. As more demands are placed on your skills and your time, it's essential that you stay on top of your game.

We've looked at all the aspects of daily office life for the administrative professional and have come up with strategic, practical and easy-to-implement solutions for the most pressing concerns.

To make it easier on you, we divided this report into four central categories integral to every administrative professional's career:

✔ **Productivity**
✔ **Organization**
✔ **Office Politics**
✔ **Recognition**

You'll find dozens of timesaving tips, helpful hints and practical advice throughout this report. We interviewed experts and pored through mountains of research to bring you the best solutions to your biggest challenges.

II. Productivity

Cultivate Creativity in a Changing Workplace

There's no way around it—you live in a constantly changing world. You spend your days working with bosses who want results yesterday, in companies that are downsizing and outsourcing, in a world where information technology is moving faster than many of us can keep up with.

As an administrative professional, you find new and more complex projects are being hurled at you while you receive little or no new training. It seems you are often expected to know everything as if by telepathy. How are you supposed to get everything done and still leave the office on time? And without sacrificing quality or your sanity in the process?

Relax. Here are several easy-to-use tips you can use *right now* to streamline your workload and improve your efficiency, even with tighter budgets and fewer resources. Remember, the goal is to have a smooth workday so you can have a smooth evening at home.

The Do's and Don'ts of Tighter Budgets

In times of tight budgets, everyone must focus on keeping the lid on spending. Although many of the cost-saving ideas that management implements appear to be ridiculous (*"What do you mean we're spending too much on paper clips?"*), the bottom line is that you can't afford to ignore the attitude driving the ideas. Some managers may take cost cutting too far—in your opinion—but you must adopt at least some form of a penny-pinching mind-set. Let's just call it being thrifty. Here are the do's and don'ts of working with tighter budgets:

DON'T fail to support or implement cost-cutting directives from above. It is in your best interest to play along.

DON'T let your co-workers know that you think some cost-cutting directives are stupid or ill-advised. Remember, you're in a respected position in the company—other employees follow your example. If you make it known that you disagree with the top brass, word will get around. Your co-workers may even view your comments as a green light to ignore cost-cutting efforts. That can't be good for anyone.

DON'T view cost-cutting incentives as temporary measures. The so-called decadent 80's are long gone, and dollar-watchers will keep watching. Cost-cutting is here to stay.

DO make your support known. When a higher-up initiates a cost-cutting incentive, do your part to announce it, support it, monitor and maintain it. Supporting upper management's ideas is not—very often—optional.

DO keep emotions out of the process. It doesn't matter if you really dislike the policy—you must keep your feelings to yourself. This is no different from any other aspect of your job you might not like—it's still essential that you remain professional.

DO look for new ways to cut costs. No matter what their position in the company, all employees should seek opportunities to save money. As an administrative professional, your role is important because you often are the person who orders office supplies for your department. If you make a conscious effort to look for the best prices and save where you can, you will win the hearts of upper management.

MAKE THE MOST OF FEWER RESOURCES

Elizabeth's boss, John, informed her that she needed to learn a new spreadsheet program. Yet when she asked for authorization to buy tutorial software, her request was turned down flat. Then, John assigned her extra projects but refused to pay for overtime or hire an assistant to help her complete them. And he needs them right away.

Welcome to corporate America. It may not always make a lot of sense, and it can be very challenging—personally and professionally. What does that mean for you? Like Elizabeth, you have to think on your feet constantly and find creative ways to work brilliantly with fewer resources. Here are five ways you can do more with less:

1. Cultivate partnerships. OK, so your boss won't let you hire an assistant, what should you do? See if you can partner with a colleague

Improve Your Writing Instantly

Do you agonize over writing business memos, letters or proposals? Perhaps you spend more time staring at the keyboard than actually using it because you don't think you know how to write well.

Here's a way to improve your writing instantly: Imagine that the person to whom you are writing is sitting with you at your kitchen table. What would you say to her? That's it. Now, write it.

The trick is to write just like you speak. You may have learned in school that you're supposed to use "big words" and sound very formal, but that's just plain wrong. Not if you want to be understood—quickly. The point is to communicate with ease.

We're all busy, and you don't want to make people get their dictionaries out just to read your memo. Keep it simple, keep it short and to the point, keep it easy—don't make writing harder than it really is.

and share the extra workload. Chances are, you each have skills to offer the other that can improve efficiency and make it so you can each accomplish more in a day.

2. Become an expert planner. The more lead time you have, the better your chances for finishing a project on your own, without having to work overtime or take work home. For example, when you know one of your assignments has a due date months away, you can begin using your spare time (like waiting in line, commuting on the subway or waiting for co-workers to show up for the weekly staff meeting) to squeeze in small bits of the project. You may even complete it before deadline and feel as if it were almost effortless. (There's more on using your time to your advantage on page 11.)

3. Think creatively. The boss says you can't have a company-sponsored holiday party because it costs too much. You can organize a potluck or collect a few dollars from everyone to make it happen. Need computer training on the latest software but have very little funding for it? Make a deal with the in-house computer expert to run learning sessions during lunch hours or before the normal workday begins. These are unusual times that require unusual ideas. Use them, as long as they don't offend or alienate you from your boss.

4. Have a good sense of humor. You've just found out no one in your department is allowed to order more paper clips—*you've already used your allotment for the month.* What do you do? Laugh. Don't get angry at this absurdity, just shrug it off and laugh about it. You'll feel better and you'll set a better example. And then figure out a way to work around it by starting an officewide recycling effort.

5. Know that you cannot do everything. At least not up to your standards and within reasonable time constraints. Something has to give. It shouldn't always be your personal interests or your peace of mind. Once you come to the realization that you can't possibly get everything done that you need to get done, you can achieve a calmness and coolheadedness that will help you through each stressful day. If you spend each day doing the best you can, then you're doing all you can do. No one can reasonably ask for more than that. Remember, you are just *one* person.

MAKE WORK INTERRUPTIONS WORK FOR YOU

As an administrative professional, you are the "answer person" and everyone in your office knows that. You dispense information, distribute supplies, offer help, give advice and solve problems. The biggest drawback? You're interrupted five million times a day by colleagues, by staff, by nearly every single person in the office at one time or another. How on earth are you to get any of your own work done, without being rude or staying at the office late into the evening?

There *is* a way to put your own priorities first and still find time to help others in the office. The key is to have a strategy, and that's where we can help. Here's how to handle with grace all the interruptions you get in a day, manage to get your own job done well and even turn many of those interruptions to your advantage:

Put your needs first. In other words, set aside a specific amount of time each day for your own work. You'll never get away with blocking out each afternoon, so don't even try. Aim low, maybe an hour or two a day, to get your own work organized and accomplish your top priorities. Once you have time designated for you, hide. Go into your boss's office and lock the door while she's in a meeting, use the cafeteria outside of lunch hours, use an empty desk in the corner. The point is to get away from everyone so you can have real quiet time for you. If you set aside more than an hour or two, you risk alienating your co-workers, so keep it brief, but make it essential.

Don't kid yourself. As nice as it may sound, you won't be able to erase interruptions from your day completely and you shouldn't—*they're a vital part of office life*. Your boss and co-workers need your help just as you need their cooperation. All offices operate on that type of give-and-take philosophy; it's how work often gets done. When you are interrupted, accept it gracefully, quickly gauge the level of your involvement needed, decide whether you can or should take the time necessary to resolve it immediately and, if not, offer a specific time and place to handle it.

Let your body do the talking. There are things you can do to discourage casual interruptions. For example, making eye contact with someone suggests that you are available for discussion. Many people will take that opportunity to offer greetings and perhaps raise subjects to you that would not have come up otherwise. If you reduce the chance for eye contact, you will reduce the number of such casual interruptions. You can do so by positioning your desk and chair so you face away from the door or passageway. If you can't do that, remain busy and avoid looking at anyone passing unless you are willing to be interrupted. Those who really do need to talk to you will knock or otherwise get your attention. Once contact has been made and the conversation begins, you can stand up to indicate gently you want to make the meeting brief.

GET TECHNOLOGICALLY SAVVY, *NOW*

Office technology, including computers, e-mail and sophisticated phone systems, offers great opportunities to get your work done faster and easier. Many companies have invested in office technology, but it is up to each employee to make the most of that investment. How can you get up to speed quickly? Here are some quick ways. (Already know the basics? Skip to page 9.)

Ask the in-house computer expert. Your company's systems manager may do more than keep the computer system humming. He may also be responsible for instructing staff on computer use. Ask. If that is not part of his job description, move to plan B—ask him if he can tutor you after work or during your lunch hour. Nearly everyone who works in an IS (Information Systems) department can tell you more about computers just off the top of their head than you'll ever want to know in your lifetime. You may need to buy him lunch if he's not on the clock or trade your editing or typing services to help you get the basics down.

Get your boss to spring for a class. It's often the quickest, best way to learn a new program or software. The Yellow Pages lists plenty of qualified instructors—most at reasonable prices.

Use the technology. The best training in the world won't help if you don't put it to use quickly. Make a point of considering how the technology available to you could make each project go faster and easier, then find out how to do it. Even if it takes a little longer the first time or two, you'll learn more about the technology and reap the rewards on future projects.

The Downside of E-mail

It can't compare to the human touch—like the occasional phone call or meeting. Make sure you use e-mail as a way to supplement other means of communication (like getting together for lunch), especially when it comes to keeping up contacts and staying in touch with colleagues.

Your tone can be misinterpreted. There are no other clues as to how you are communicating, such as body language, and your message can be misinterpreted. Before you hit that "send" button, take a minute to review your message for possible misinterpretation of intent, overall tone and errors. Remember that anything you write could end up on the boss's desk.

E-mail is not private. Not even close, as a matter of fact. You should always assume that anything you write in an e-mail can become public knowledge—never, ever disclose confidential or personal information in your e-mail exchanges. Besides being careful about the content of your messages, you should also make it a habit to delete messages regularly from your in and out boxes (mail received and mail sent) to keep the "snoopers" at bay. (You can always save important messages on a disk—and off your hard drive.)

It's not foolproof. Messages get lost from time to time, so be sure to use other methods of follow-up on important projects.

Strike the Right Balance Between Your Work and Personal Life

You are more than your work. To find the right balance of work and personal life for you, without the quality of either suffering, use these guidelines:

1. Make sure your professional and personal goals are compatible. As each of us moves through our life, our needs change. For example, if we have young children or aging relatives to care for, the demands on our personal time and energy will be much higher than at other times, and we must reduce our work goals accordingly. At other times, we can devote more to our work and those goals can be raised. Look at your needs and goals carefully—and realistically. Set professional and personal goals that will meet your most important needs and work to meet them. Just as important, review your goals on a regular basis and change them as your circumstances change.

2. Set a home agenda, too. If your organized workday dissolves into chaos when you get home, it can cause you headaches and make you feel like you don't have any spare time. That, in turn, can affect your work life. Here's an easy solution: Make a to-do list for your home, much like the one for work. When you come home from work, ask each family member what he or she would like to accomplish with you during the evening. Maybe there's a special television show one of your children would really like to watch, or perhaps he or she needs help with a school assignment. Make a list of their wishes and mesh them with your own needs, then share the miniagenda with your family, and go from there. For younger children, be sure to include bedtime on the agenda every day. And don't forget to include quiet time.

3. Put emergency plans in place. It *will* happen. You will be called away from work to handle an emergency: to pick up your child from school one day or be out of the office to care for a sick relative. You must have plans in place at work to cover your absence. Perhaps a trusted colleague would be willing to "swap" responsibilities with you—when either of you needs to be out of the office. This person can handle your *must-do* tasks, and when that colleague is out of the office, you return the favor. You should also have projects on hand that you can work on from home during those times you can't be in the office, but would be able to do a little work anyway, such as perusing your reading file, learning software programs or updating your contact information.

4. Be realistic. Trying to fit in both a demanding work life and a busy personal life can be almost overwhelming. When promotions or new assignments arise, the challenge to balance it all becomes even greater. When you are spending a great deal of time at the office, talk with your loved ones about their expectations and how you can spend time together around your work schedule. Let them know why work is important to you and how they benefit from it. If you aren't spending as much time as you would like with those you care for, discuss your personal and professional goals with your boss to see if the two of you can work out a plan to your mutual benefit.

5. Show your family how much you care about them. Sending flowers to a loved one, putting special notes in with your children's

---

More Help in Emergencies

Many companies are finding that providing emergency backup child care is just what the doctor ordered. When the nanny is ill or school is closed, on-site child care centers can provide a safety net for parents who cannot miss work.

When an emergency occurs, instead of taking a vacation day or calling in sick, the parent can leave the child in good hands at the company-run child care center and spend a productive day in the office. The cost to the companies is low, especially when you compare it to the benefits— reduced absenteeism, increased loyalty, lower employee turnover, improved productivity and higher morale.

If your company has not yet looked into the benefits of having a child care facility on-site, do some background research, go through it with your boss and encourage her to pursue it further. It shouldn't hurt to make a suggestion, especially when it concerns what's best for the company on a long-term basis, and there are several case studies available where companies, even as small as 60 employees, have successfully established on-site child care programs for their employees. Good sources for information are the Internet and your local bookstore and library.

Keep Your Friendships Fresh and Rewarding

Finding it difficult to squeeze even your closest friends into the picture? Mix it up: Invite your best friend along when running errands. Time together on even the most routine of tasks, like grocery shopping, can help keep friendships strong.

Source: Stephanie Winston's *Best Organizing Tips*. Available at your local bookstore.

lunches, or making dates with your family members are all ways you can show them how important they are to you. Remember, a little bit goes a long way—you spend a minimal amount of time (like dashing off a note to your son, for instance) to make a big difference in someone's day.

FITTING IT ALL IN

You've read about all the do's and don'ts of tighter budgets, how to work brilliantly with fewer resources, how to handle interruptions and even turn them to your advantage, how to boost your technological savvy—*quickly* and how to balance your work and home life. How do you fit it all in? You won't ever feel as if you have enough time, but you can feel better about spending the time you have. How do you move from *knowing* what to do to taking action? The answer—one step at a time.

It's a basic aspect of today's office—you won't ever have enough time. You have to take large projects or goals and break them up into manageable pieces. Instead of panicking over all the computer stuff you don't know, plan on learning a little bit, day by day. You don't have to become an expert in one fell swoop—it won't happen that way anyway. Make the most of the extra five minutes you have before that staff meeting, or the 10 minutes you have left before your lunch hour, to expand your knowledge or improve your productivity.

III. ORGANIZATION

FINE-TUNE YOUR SKILLS TO IMPROVE EFFICIENCY

Organization is not an end result. It's more of a work in progress, a way of life. Everyone—from the top brass' assistant to entry-level administrative professionals—should continually fine-tune their organizational skills.

It's even more important today that you stay on top of your organizing. You're asked to add more complex items to your to-do list and expected to be even more productive with even fewer resources. Your desk seems littered with new piles of work every time you turn around.

We'll show you how to get it all done, without spending more time at the office. We'll tell you how the pros set priorities, how they juggle multiple projects and easy ways to retrieve any file—*instantly*. We'll show you the best ways to purge your files and *never* miss a deadline or a detail. And if you work with someone who can't manage his time, we'll show you how to deal with that, too.

PRIORITIZE LIKE A PRO

Everyone is very fond of telling you that you need to set priorities in order to improve your efficiency in the workplace. The problem is, most of those same people won't tell you how to go about setting priorities, that is, not anything that you can really use. They won't tell you, for example, what to do when *everything* is a priority, or when one boss says her project is more important than another boss's project. But we'll tell it to you straight, right here, right now. Here's all you need to know about setting priorities:

1. Make a list of everything you need to accomplish. This isn't your ordinary to-do list—this is a master list of everything from daily tasks to monthly projects to special assignments coming up in the year ahead. It will give you a broad, overarching view of how your time is going to be spent. Don't let this list intimidate you by its size—think of it as an essential ingredient to being organized. You will soon break it down and work on it in manageable pieces.

2. Divide the projects on the list into three categories:

Group One:

Urgent "must-do-right-now" tasks. Tasks such as photocopying the speech your boss is giving tomorrow morning or getting that proposal to the client by noon.

High-stress tasks, or ones requiring special concentration. Examples would be preparing a presentation for your boss, or setting up the company picnic plans.

Bonus tasks. Tasks your boss didn't ask you to do, but you know will make a good impression if you take the initiative to do them. Examples are checking out cost-cutting software or doing research on the competition.

Group Two:

Day-to-day tasks. These tasks include daily duties such as preparing the agenda for the weekly staff meeting or scheduling appointments for your boss.

Group Three:

Routine tasks. These are tasks you do nearly every day, such as filing, sorting mail, setting up reading files, checking your e-mail.

3. Take action. Now that you know how to categorize what you need to accomplish, you can see the logical order in which to do them. Work on your Group One tasks first, during the time of day when you feel most productive. Group Two and Three tasks can be tackled after you've finished Group One tasks or when you need a break from them. The goal is to personalize the system and make it yours—even if it means changing the system we present here.

WHAT IF *EVERYTHING* IS A PRIORITY?

Some days just seem to be out of control. Your boss wants everything done yesterday ... your colleagues need your help—*now* ... everyone wants just a "minute" of your time ... and you have a million items on your to-do list that have to be done *right now*. What do you do?

Look closely at deadlines. For example, you've got two projects with identical deadlines—writing a report for your boss and preparing his agenda for the meeting in an hour. Although you listed them due at the same time, you may have more "wiggle room" than you thought. Discuss the deadlines with your boss. If the report is not needed until the afternoon, work on the morning agenda first.

If your boss says the report needs to be done immediately, along with the agenda, ask a colleague if you can have some of her help to meet your dual deadlines. If you do this sparingly and with a reciprocal agreement—when she's on deadline and in a crunch—it can go a long way toward controlling your work life and getting you out of the office at a reasonable hour.

Take a hard look at your competing priorities. Everything must be done but there's not enough time to do it all. Ask yourself, what will happen if I don't do this? Gauging the consequences of not completing the work will help you decide among even the toughest of priorities.

Talk to your boss. He has initially set your priorities for getting your work done. But if you run into conflicting priorities and feel you need his input before resolving them, ask him.

ARE YOU ORGANIZED? A SHORT QUIZ

Answer the following questions "yes" or "no" to get a quick assessment of just how organized you are.

1. Do you keep a daily to-do list and cross off items as you complete them?

2. Do you schedule weekly meetings with your boss(es) to review the status of the workload, update each other, discuss objectives, set priorities, give and get feedback and express your concerns?

3. If you have more than one boss, do you have structures for prioritizing their work?

4. Have you established a procedure for covering the bases when you're unavailable?

5. Do you make effective use of support systems—messengers, temps, junior administrative professionals and interns—to handle emergencies and other overloads?

6. Is your filing system meeting your current needs? Can you retrieve what you need immediately?

7. Are you making effective use of calendars, either electronic or paper, for noting and tracking appointments and meetings and staying on schedule?

8. Do you and your boss set realistic deadlines? Do you schedule checkpoints where both of you can assess how projects are going?

9. Do you have a practical method for managing interruptions, such as asking some callers to call back later, asking them to e-mail you or instructing the receptionist to hold calls during crunch periods?

10. Do you group tasks that can easily overlap, e.g., dropping off a report on the way to lunch or reading while waiting for a meeting to begin?

11. Do you know your limits and heed signals that it's time to take a break, change tasks or enlist assistance?

12. Do you break problems into manageable pieces to handle in small steps?

Unless you could honestly answer "yes" to every question, you have room to improve your organizational skills. The following pages will lay the groundwork for organizing your work and controlling the chaos.

FILE REVIEW: RETRIEVE ANYTHING—INSTANTLY

Your boss rushes to your desk and needs the file on the Johnson account immediately. Do you know where it is? Exactly? Can you hand it to her while she's breathing down your neck? Or do you have to tell her that you will locate it and track her down as soon as possible?

You'll make a great impression if you can retrieve that file instantly for your boss. You know that. But if you don't have a filing system that makes it that easy, implement these simple systems, as recommended by top organizational expert Stephanie Winston.

1. The umbrella principle: Use very general category headings for your file folders. The key is to think in terms of functionality. If you have several folders—salaries, goals, expenditures, etc.—pertaining to the 2002 budget, file them under—*you guessed it*—"Budget 2002." With a broad heading like that, you'll know that anything pertaining to the budget will be in that section. If it becomes too full, break it out into two folders, using the general title with a different subhead for each folder.

2. The sponge principle: When naming your file folders, use headings that will absorb, spongelike, substantial amounts of paper. Instead of filing a handful of promotional mailings from one competitor in one folder, designate a bigger folder to "Competition" or "Industry News."

3. The noun principle: Don't use adjectives to describe your files, like "New Ad Campaigns." By the time you find that file, the campaign may not be new anymore. Do use nouns, such as "Ad Campaigns, 2001, East Coast" or "National Ad Campaigns, 2003."

Once you've got a good system in place for easy retrieval, fine-tune it. For example, color coding your files is a great way to organize within your organizing. One administrative professional for a publishing company uses a different color for each of the newsletters it publishes. Another administrative professional assigns each person in her department a different color folder.

Folders should be organized as "working,"—or "hot"—files and "reference" files, which are used less frequently and don't necessarily have to be within arm's reach. Here are more tips from Stephanie Winston:

Referral files: Quick-reference folders that you set up to hold information pertaining only to your boss and colleagues. For example, you will meet with a junior administrative professional about how she can manage her career. Start a file with her name on it. As you come across articles or paperwork that could help her, toss it in her folder and pull it for the meeting.

Holding files: Your follow-up file for all paperwork related to current projects requiring future, but not instant, action.

Action files: Your to-do list in a folder. For example, if researching industry news for your boss is at the top of your to-do list, throw your trade journals or industry publications into a folder and you've got an action file. You may not want to keep your action files in file folders at all—many administrative professionals prefer to use their in-box as an action file. The point is not to let it fall off your radar. By filing all items into a folder or an in-box, you won't lose sight of the details.

Is E-mail Filing Different From Paper Filing?

No. It's not different at all. Treat e-mail as if it were a piece of paper, cluttering your desktop. Review each e-mail and take some type of action, either delete, forward or save it in an electronic "file cabinet" for action at a later date. Don't let e-mail pile up, and act on it as soon as possible.

Hot files: The files you refer to daily, even hourly. Hot files must be kept close by, you may need them at a moment's notice. Use either a "hot" file desk or cabinet drawer within arm's reach or a file folder rack on your desktop.

5 SECRETS TO BETTER ORGANIZATION

1. If it works, don't worry about how it looks. As long as your filing system works for you, it's really a matter of your personal style. Some people are neat and orderly, others have cluttered desks and messy offices. Both can be organized, despite their obvious differences. Some people with incredibly cluttered desks can retrieve files faster than someone who's tidy.

2. Organize your files around retrieval. Easy retrieval is the goal of any worthwhile filing system. If you can't find it, you might as well not have it.

3. Assign toss-out dates to your files. If you never throw anything away, you'll make the filing cabinet manufacturers very happy, but your retrieval process will suffer. You simply don't need to keep every piece of paper forever. For general rules about how long you should keep certain documents, see page 19.

4. Move your paper—don't let it pile up. To avoid huge piles of paper on your desk, make it a habit to go through the paper that lands on your desk several times a week. Start at the top of the pile and do something—*anything*—with it. Give it to your boss, throw it away, file it away, reply to it immediately. If you can't do anything with it at the moment, place it in a holding file, assign it a date and handle it later. Continue through your stack of papers until you've found a place for each piece.

5. Clear your desk before you leave for the day. It can be so disheartening to walk into your office every morning only to see a disaster piled atop your desk. Before you leave each night, stack files neatly, put away items that don't need to be on your desktop (paper clips, folders or notebooks), throw away trash (like the paper cup still sitting on your desk from that coffee eight hours earlier) and turn your desk into a pleasant working area. Even if you thrive in a more cluttered environment, it's still nice to start fresh each morning with a clear (or uncomplicated) desktop.

LEARN TO PURGE YOUR PAPER FILES

How long do you need to keep files or documents? Some documents must be kept specified lengths of time for legal or financial reasons. Others are kept solely at the company's discretion. If your company has record-retention policies, you should know and follow them. If not, you may want to recommend that your company adopt some, with assistance from legal and accounting personnel. Here are some general guidelines:

Tax/financial records: Many experts recommend you keep all documentation concerning your company's accounting, sales and tax records for seven years, in case of an IRS audit.

Other experts cut that time to four years, the same amount of time the IRS uses for its statutes of limitations. We recommend you keep these documents longer than the experts suggest—the IRS can review your records as far back as it deems necessary. It's not likely, but it is possible.

Employment records: The Fair Labor Standards Act (FLSA) requires companies to keep records for each employee concerning payroll, collective bargaining agreements, employment contracts, wage rates, work schedules and timecards—for the duration of their employment. If an employee leaves the company, keep those records for at least three years after departure, in case employment-related issues arise later.

OSHA: The Occupational Safety and Health Administration (OSHA) requires that medical records for workers who have been exposed to hazardous substances be kept for the duration of their employment, plus 30 years. Records of occupational-related illnesses or injuries must be kept for five years.

Benefits records: The Employee Retirement Income Security Act (ERISA) requires companies to keep documentation concerning pension contributions, employee years of service and pension benefits permanently.

General correspondence: Paperwork that does not fall into the above category should be destroyed after a set period of time (for example, two years). Any document that needs to be kept longer should be clearly marked with a "Destroy on XX/XX/XX" note.

KEEP TRACK OF THE DEADLINES AND THE DETAILS

Mary, a hard-working administrative professional, has been losing sleep worrying about whether she has forgotten some important detail in the crush of the workday. Often, she tosses and turns, reviewing the day's events again and again. Other nights, she sleeps, only to bolt upright in bed, remembering a detail that fell through the cracks.

She turned to a colleague, Grace, for advice. Grace gave Mary some tips to use immediately to keep track of all the details.

Instead of jotting notes on yellow Post-it notes or scraps of paper, as Mary liked to do, Grace suggested she buy a calendar/planner and use it to track both her daily to-do list and her yearlong master list. Mary would add new tasks to her list as they were assigned, as well as ideas or project notes she wanted to keep track of.

Grace also suggested Mary might want to "go electronic." Many organizations use companywide electronic calendars that also function as planners. Mary began using software to keep track of all the details in her professional and personal life, reserving the personal data on her own computer while making the professional data available to her co-workers over the company network.

MANAGING A POOR TIME MANAGER

Your boss just cannot get it together when it comes to managing his time. He is always late for meetings, cannot seem to make decisions quickly and doesn't churn out projects in a timely manner. In short, he's making both of you look bad. What can you do?

The first step is to know with whom you are dealing. For example, is your boss the type who likes to wait until the last possible minute on every project, or is he someone who can't keep track of details? By knowing your boss's type, you can complement his work style and minimize the number of crises you need to deal with. We've included descriptions of a few of the most common types of manager work styles. And, because you probably won't be able to change your boss's habits, we've also included some secrets for working successfully with each type of manager.

The cliffhanger. This individual likes to wait until the last possible moment to deliver a finished project. He thrives on the pressure of a looming deadline and will create that pressure if it isn't there already. Constant reminders from you about an upcoming project will likely just be a source of frustration for you. Better to do what you can to minimize the effect the looming crisis will have on you. For example, do what you can in advance to prepare for the coming "crunch" (gather necessary documents, make preliminary phone calls, etc.). If nothing else, try to arrange your work to leave extra open time to devote to the crisis when it erupts—it might get you home earlier.

The allergic-to-details type. Lots of bosses are famous for ignoring details—that's why they have assistants, right? If you are working for this type of manager, realize that you will have to keep track of her job and yours. Keep files on her projects that include the kinds of details that she is likely to need in the future. It'll save you from a mad rush to reconstruct information later.

The fence sitter. You'd never know that decision making is part of a manager's job the way some bosses wallow in indecision. If possible, you may want to help your fence-sitting boss subtly by suggesting intermediate decision points during a project. Dealing with just part of the project at one time may make it easier for your boss to reach decisions and keep the project moving. At the very least, you should anticipate an unusually high number of meetings and probable delays as your boss wrestles with major decisions, and plan your workload accordingly.

The hopper. This individual typically has an unusually high energy level and a curious mind. He tends to jump from one project to another without necessarily finishing any of them. Your first goal should be to understand your boss's agenda and adjust your work to match his. You can sometimes do this through experience with your boss's work patterns or by looking for clues from conversations, requests, meetings, etc. If necessary, arrange with your boss to discuss his agenda—on a daily basis if necessary. Your second goal should be to try bringing some projects to closure. If closure requires just a few more steps that you can easily do yourself, consider taking the initiative to do so. It will make your boss and you look good. If not, try to find ways to subtly suggest ways the boss can bring closure before moving to the next project. For example, you might say, "Perhaps Joe could call the vendor and make the final arrangements now that you've decided what we need."

The perfectionist. This boss can easily drive you crazy, spending her time correcting others' less-than-perfect work and agreeing to take on any and all projects (after all, no one can do them better than she can). Not only are you likely to receive your share of criticism and correction for your work, her workload is likely to become your workload as she takes on more and more. Your best protection in this case is a clear standard of performance that both you and your boss can agree to. Otherwise, nothing you do will ever be quite good enough. Also, after ensuring that you are indeed being as productive and attentive to priorities as possible, you need to place the responsibility for prioritizing work where it belongs—with your boss. If she gives you more to do than is reasonable in the time you have to do it, she needs to decide whether to get extra help or give up some of the work. This can be hard to do, but failure to do so can make your job even harder.

IV. OFFICE POLITICS

THE IMPORTANCE OF KNOWING THE GAME

You may not like to think about "office politics," but it exists in every office. There are rules and territories that are as real as they are unspoken. As an administrative professional, you are on the front line, interacting with many of the key players in the office. If you use office politics to your advantage, you can gain allies and cooperation in your quest to control the chaos. The problem is, you are left to learn the rules yourself. In the pages that follow, we'll reveal "insider" secrets and unspoken rules no one else will tell you.

Whether you're just getting started on your career, or you're interested in fine-tuning your skills in today's ever-changing work place, these practical, easy-to-use tips will help.

10 SECRETS TO MASTERING OFFICE POLITICS

1. Stay positive. A pleasant disposition will get you everywhere. Even on those really hectic days when the last thing on your mind is spreading good cheer, keep in mind that people are always watching you. It's important to move your negative thoughts to a back burner and smile in the face of chaos.

2. Choose your words wisely. Make sure the words and phrases you choose reflect your upbeat attitude and team player philosophy. Negative remarks, even casual ones, will be remembered far more accurately—and for a lot longer—than all the positive ones you make. For some examples of phrases to avoid—and we've included some that will surprise you—see page 25.

3. Listen well. *Always* keep your ears open. You never know what you'll hear. The better listener you are, the more productive and effective employee you will be. So listen well, not only to your bosses and colleagues to prevent miscommunication but also to "sour apples," so you'll know who to avoid allying with.

4. Don't sling mud. Once words are spoken, or written, it's difficult to take them back. Count to 10 before you speak. Take a walk around the block. Excuse yourself to go to the restroom. No matter how much you may personally dislike a boss or colleague, keep those thoughts to yourself—it's not only unprofessional to cut someone down, it can hamper your success at work. And it sure isn't very nice either. If you need to vent, write about it in your journal at home, or talk with someone outside the office—as long as it doesn't betray confidences or risk making its way back to work.

When a new employee starts, make the person feel welcome. The smallest gestures on your part go a long way. For example, spending 10 minutes showing the new hire around the office, making introductions, pointing out restrooms, kitchens and supply cabinets will endear you to him forever.

5. Don't burn bridges—*no matter how tempting.* No one gets to the top alone, so make sure you don't forget all the people you have met along the way. If you appreciate and understand the importance of their role in your life, you will have a stronger network of supportive, encouraging allies.

6. Networking is key. We all need friends and allies in our corner, supplying us with information, assistance, job leads, support, quick answers, encouragement, advice, insight and inspiration. If you've got a strong network, you've got a powerful resource. You're more likely to have the positions and work life you really want.

7. Salute the general. Part of your job as an administrative professional is to make your boss look good. It's up to you to set the tone for the office by showing respect for the boss's position and authority.

8. Stay on top of your game. The competition for the best jobs is intense. You must update old skills and learn new ones constantly to maintain your value in the workplace. Read professional newsletters and books, take courses, consult online resources and keep an open mind to new and better ways of working.

9. Display grace under pressure. Offices will get even busier, more demands will be made upon you, pressure will increase. If you blow your top, you won't survive. Make a habit of donning "your professional face" and letting things go.

10. Think money. Always keep your eye on the bottom line: That's what your boss is doing. Seek ways to cut costs, beat the budget and increase profit. If you keep your eye on the money, you'll always win the hearts of management.

ENSURE YOUR SUCCESS

Now that you know the unspoken rules of the political game, here's a primer on other key political points you need to know.

1. Play positive office politics. Search out opportunities to turn co-workers into allies. Expanding your sphere of influence or your network of supporters is key to getting your work done faster, easier and getting home at a reasonable hour. Of course, these arrangements should be to your mutual benefit. Take on extra assignments, even the boring ones. Offer to assist a colleague working under the crush of a deadline. Help where you can, and where you cannot, refer your co-worker to someone who can. Use your accumulated influence to gath-

---

Avoid phrases such as, "I can't help you," or "I don't have time." They send a message to your boss and colleagues that you aren't a team player and that you aren't a good time manager. You can't allow constant interruptions, but you can offer conciliatory statements such as, "let me finish this memo, and I'll make time to lend a hand," or "I'm on deadline right now, but why don't you let me ask Joanne to help you."

---

er information, add allies and make your job easier.

2. Be a team player. Offices are collaborations of people working together to achieve common goals. If you disrupt the flow of information exchange, or grumble loudly when asked for help, you risk alienating yourself from your co-workers. It's important to put aside personal differences or issues for the good of the whole. Being a team player means doing what you can to help, whenever you can—*even if it means temporarily setting aside your own work.* You may need their help later.

3. Think ahead. Always look for ways to get your office's work done faster and easier. At the very least, try to anticipate problems and prevent them from growing into needless disasters that absorb tremendous time and energy. Forward-thinkers accomplish more in less time simply because they are always on the lookout for ways to get ahead of the game.

WORKING EFFECTIVELY FOR MULTIPLE BOSSES

Today, many administrative professionals report to more than one boss. Multiple bosses can mean more complexity and conflicting priorities in your work.

Ultimately, it is the responsibility of your bosses to set the overall priorities for the work you do. Your responsibility is to work productively and creatively within the overall priorities your bosses have set. If you can't avoid violating the priorities and deadlines you have been given, then it is appropriate to take the matter to the bosses involved. If you do, offer whatever alternatives you can (*e.g.*, bring in additional help, work overtime, put one job ahead of the other) and leave it for them to decide.

A good filing system is especially important when tracking work for multiple bosses. See page 16 for more on effective filing systems.

HOW DO YOU TELL YOUR BOSS HE'S WRONG?

The answer: V-v-v-e-e-e-r-r-r-y-y-y carefully.

In fact, it's better to tell him how right you are without telling him how wrong he is. No one likes to hear they're wrong. You need to tread lightly.

Here's how you present your ideas:

- Tailor your idea so your boss can approve it without involving a higher authority.

- Buttress your proposal with guidelines spelled out in company policy.

- Stress cost savings, speed and quality. Ideas that promise to improve all three have a far better chance of acceptance.
- Show how the change will make your boss look good and the company more profitable or reputable.
- Test your idea with staff members who would be affected by it, to gain their support. If you're going to meet a hard-to-persuade boss's objection that "others on the staff won't like it," this is an essential step.
- Use company jargon and terms that are popular with top management.
- Give three reasons why your idea should be accepted.

LEARN TO SAY "NO"—AND DELIGHT YOUR BOSS

Sarah reports to four bosses. Sometimes it is difficult for her to set boundaries with each. Although they hold regular meetings to determine priorities, her bosses have short memories when it comes to her workload. Often, one of them will rush over to her desk and breathlessly insist she drop whatever she's doing and begin working on his project. Other times, each of the them will just keep dumping more and more work on her desk.

She clearly needs to say "no," in a way that is neither rude nor unprofessional. It is essential—if she doesn't say no, she'll never get anything done. She chooses her words wisely.

Another way Sarah can handle a work overload: "I'd like to be able to help you with that proposal, Jack, but I'm on deadline for one of Claire's projects right now. How about I squeeze it in just as soon as I can? Just leave the information here on my desk and I'll handle it as soon as possible." If it really is an emergency situation, Sarah and Jack should talk with Claire.

"You can check with Claire if you want me to stop working on her project now. But her deadline is earlier than yours, so instead of asking her about doing your work, why don't we see if Colleen has some time to help you. Let's go over and talk to her now."

HAVE DIFFICULT BOSSES EATING OUT OF THE PALM OF YOUR HAND

We've all had one. Or more. The boss who grabs credit where it's not due ... bullies, tyrants and taskmasters ... burned-out bosses ... game-playing bosses ... powder-keg bosses, ready to explode at any moment. It can ruin your job to work with a difficult boss ... at the very least you probably go home with a headache too often. Consider these pointers before you look for other employment opportunities:

Take emotions out of it. If you're frustrated at the end of the day because you think your boss doesn't like you or respect you, you need to differentiate between work relationships and personal relationships. If you let the boss "get to you" on a personal level, then the boss is manipulating you—remember, the point of a working relationship is to get the work done. Nothing more.

Be *Politely* Disagreeable

Many people get so caught up in an idea or a project they are working on that they lose their objectivity. That loss of objectivity can lead to bad decision making and poor choices. As an administrative professional, you are in a unique position to be the voice of reason ... but how you approach it, especially if it's your boss's decision you don't agree with, is key to your success. Here's how to be a reality check for your boss, or anyone else with whom you may not agree, and still maintain a healthy working relationship:

- Ask questions so you understand the idea more fully. Don't try to dissuade your boss from pursuing the objectionable idea, instead adopt a cooperative attitude by asking logical questions about the project. This approach will have one of two outcomes: Your boss will see the flaws in his design or you'll gain more respect for his idea.

- Offer ideas, support and planning assistance. Be ready to offer whatever assistance you can in restructuring or improving your boss's idea.

- Don't voice your reservation to others. Word *will* get back to your boss if you say anything negative or show your disapproval.

Don't play the boss's game. Don't stoop to his level. Instead, focus on valid work issues and remain professional at all times.

Find ways to minimize the effects of the bad behavior rather than trying to correct the behavior itself. You won't be able to turn a bully into a considerate supervisor with your reforms. You can, however, identify the negative aspects of the behavior and work to minimize the impact they have on you.

SHE'S BLAMING YOU FOR HER MISTAKE ... AGAIN

You're waiting outside your boss's door to speak with her and she motions to wait until she finishes her phone call. As you wait, you hear her say, "My assistant didn't give me the message about the meeting—I'm sorry I missed it." You know you told her about the meeting—you even watched her write it on her calendar.

She may see her action as a "little white lie" that easily gets her off the hook. You know that it conveys to others that you are not competently doing an integral part of your job. That image can hurt your reputation and even reflect badly on the boss for tolerating such incompetence. What should you do?

If you think her actions reflect poorly on your work and that they will hurt your reputation, you need to speak with her about it. Keep your cool when you tell her you've heard her blaming you for a mistake (or mistakes) you didn't make—and give examples. Explain that you understand the temptation to tell a "white lie" to avoid an embarrassing moment, but doing a good job is important to you and you feel she is damaging your reputation. Not only that, but such actions can cast a shadow over the entire office. Others will start wondering why she keeps someone working for her who is that incompetent. Ask her to stop blaming you for mistakes you have not made.

If she takes your request to heart—*congratulations!* You've started building a better—*and healthier*—working relationship with your boss. If she continues to blame you for her mistakes, you should assume there is little chance of changing her behavior. It is important to consider your options carefully based on your individual circumstances. Unfortunately, the only way to avoid permanent damage to your reputation or your psyche may be to ask for a transfer to another department or seek other employment.

Become Your Boss's Greatest Asset

Here are two ways to increase your value to your boss:

1. Become a problem-solver. Problems pop up all the time in daily business life. It's how you handle those problems that makes you stand apart from the crowd. Here are several ways you can use right now to unlock your creative thinking and earn the reputation of a creative problem-solver:

Turn the situation upside down. When you're faced with a problem that seems to have no easy answer, turn it upside down—and get a fresh perspective on it. Ask yourself, "What if this were reversed?" or, "Could some negative aspects be considered positive and vice versa?" Challenge yourself to look at the problem in ways that are innovative and creative.

Challenge your assumptions. By discarding certain assumptions, you leave your mind open to new thoughts and ideas. Ask yourself questions such as, "Does it really have to be this way?" or, "Suppose nobody had ever done this before, how would I make a fresh start?"

Tear the problem apart. Take the problem apart, piece by piece, and list the elements of it. Then review each element one by one and look for new relationships among the parts.

Rearrange it. Once you know the elements of a problem, try rearranging them in a different sequence. You may find ways to save time and money.

Find the analogy. If you can relate the problem to another situation entirely, it can help you come up with answers not available before. For example, Dr. William Harvey made medical history by explaining how the circulatory system worked: He likened the heart to a pump and gave himself a new frame of reference—and from that he understood blood vessels as part of a unified pumping system.

2. Be a stress-buster for your boss. Your boss's stress level is related to your own. When your boss is having a bad day, it can be easy for him to pass that mood along to you. But you can put a plan in place that will reduce your boss' stress and, therefore, your own. Here's how:

Anticipate your boss's needs and meet them. Review last year's calendar to determine what may come up in the next few months, then meet with your boss about what he hopes to accomplish. You can provide needed information, support, data and resources without your boss asking for it.

Present solutions rather than problems. Resist the temptation to pass all problems along to your boss. Instead, offer solutions when you inform him of problems.

Respect your boss's time. Communicate with him in a concise manner. Give him the whole picture, all relevant facts and answer his questions. Your boss will see you are saving him time, and you'll polish your image as a stress-reducer.

Use your professionalism to put your boss at ease. A confident display from you assures your boss you're in control. Psychologically, your boss needs to see that you're in control. Your calm demeanor will lower everyone's stress level.

Let your boss's attitude shape your own. Pick up on subtle cues from your boss's behavior and adopt appropriate behavior. If your boss seems unhappy or concerned, for example, take a seat and wait quietly for him to initiate conversation.

V. RECOGNITION

GET REWARDED FOR A JOB WELL DONE

Beyond your relationships with your boss and co-workers, there is one more person you need to pay close attention to each day: you. You need to look out for your own best interests, both personally and professionally, because no one else will. It's important that you promote yourself and your accomplishments to receive the recognition you deserve. You wouldn't blow your own horn every day, but there are ways—more subtle ways—to showcase your expertise and receive recognition. We'll tell you about some of them.

You're waiting for an elevator with a company executive. Do you smile and initiate a conversation? Do you make small talk? Or do you use that opportunity to talk about the good work you and your boss have recently accomplished?

Many administrative professionals would take the more passive route and keep the encounter light—and brief—if they spoke at all. Administrative professionals who work hard at promoting the work they and their bosses accomplish as a team are far more successful in their career and are happier with their work life. They understand their reputation for professionalism results, in part, from spreading good news about what they have done and that understanding goes hand-in-hand with displaying a full range of interests and talents, as well as their involvement in and concern for the company.

How do you "toot your own horn"? The key is to start talking. Get the conversational ball rolling at any opportunity, *e.g.*, waiting for the elevator or walking to the parking lot. Here are four simple ways you can use today to initiate a lively discussion that will make you look great:

1. Talk about common interests. You and the executive may both be sports fans or live on the same side of town. If you can find a bond on a personal level, it will warm the executive, making it easier for you to promote yourself.

2. Show interest in what others are doing. Congratulating a vice president on a speech well done or asking an executive how her business trip went will flatter and impress them—*and get you noticed.* People love it when someone shows interest in their activities or accomplishments. If you can sincerely praise someone's work, and if you show a genuine interest in what other people in the organization are doing, you'll come across as someone who cares a great deal for the company—and that will build your credibility and your visibility. Not only that, but keeping your finger on the pulse of the company will help you feel more comfortable and confident in your job.

5 Ways to Earn Respect, Not Blame

Your boss is accusing you of missing the deadline on an important project. But you know that you've been trying for days to get Ted in accounting to do his job, only to find out he never received the information he needed from Suzanne, who never got what she needed from Robert. You had done all you could, stopping by their desks, calling them, checking up on the progress, reminding them of deadlines. The whole process was late from the beginning, but of course you're getting blamed for it.

Here are five ways for you to regain the respect you deserve:

1. Explain what happened. Stick to the facts and don't get defensive.

2. Don't criticize or blame others. If you come down hard on Ted and Suzanne and Robert, you'll discredit yourself by looking negative. And when they hear what you've done, they'll be reluctant to help you again when you really need it.

3. Keep emotions separate. You're probably angry at being accused, but don't show it. Despite the difficulty, keep your calm, your voice level, and remember that it's not personal.

4. Accept responsibility for your role in the missed deadline. When a deadline is missed or something goes awry, it usually involves several people, including you.

5. Offer to help fix it. The deadline has passed, but a phone call from you to the printer may buy more time. Let your boss know you're willing to do what you can.

3. Talk about the work you and your boss are doing. Sharing interesting information is one way to connect with others and make them more receptive to sharing news with you. For example, if you know an executive who is interested in a speech your boss is giving, strike up a conversation about the group your boss is addressing and tell him about the background research you've conducted.

4. Mention pertinent industry news or information that you've heard. This is a clear sign of your professionalism and your smarts—showing you're knowledgeable and interested in what the organization is doing and where it's headed. It shows you're career-minded, not just job-oriented.

ASK FOR A RAISE IN THIS PENNY-PINCHING ERA? YOU BETCHA!

Asking for and receiving a raise is one of the most difficult business issues you'll encounter. Not only do you and your supervisor assess your job performance, but you discuss money—something most of us dislike doing.

Asking for a raise demonstrates two important qualities: your initiative and your pride in your work. The key to receiving one is to ask in just the right way. You must have a well-planned strategy, which offers tangible work-related reasons that warrant a raise and a realistic picture of how you will continue to benefit your boss and the company in the future.

Here's your five-step plan to get your raise:

Step 1: Know your market value. Research administrative salaries in your geographical area. Ask around your network for typical salary ranges (including benefits and perks). Call employment agencies and review employment ads in the paper. Gather "inside information" about your company's policy on raises (if the average raise last year was 4 percent, it's usually not realistic to expect 10 percent this year) and its financial situation.

Step 2: Present a solid record of your accomplishments and rely on it as your key negotiation tool. Avoid saying, "I have bills to pay," or, "I've demonstrated good work and I deserve a raise." While they may be true, they are not generally relevant. It's your track record and value to the firm that you should emphasize instead.

Step 3: Present complimentary letters, citations and other forms of recognition from clients, colleagues and customers to bolster your position. Your boss has a lot of things on his mind... he may need more of a reminder about just how good you are.

Step 4: Keep your tone positive when you meet with the boss. Present your raise as a win-win situation: You've demonstrated your professionalism; more money will help you devote even more energy and enthusiasm to your work.

Step 5: Let your boss name a dollar figure first. If it's more than you had hoped for, accept it graciously and without showing surprise. If it's less, start negotiating. You know your market value, so you'll know if the offer falls into the acceptable range.

The U.S. Bureau of Labor Statistics can provide you with data to compare your salary and benefits to others inside and outside of your industry. Visit its Web site at www.bls.gov. By doing a quick check, you'll be in a better position to negotiate.

If your attempts with your boss are less than successful, don't give up. Instead, talk to your boss about your goals and your position in the company—where you would like to go, how you should go about getting there. Ask for specific steps you can take to succeed in your salary negotiations the next time around. Ask for a date to approach your boss again. Mark it in your calendar and start planning to accomplish your new goals.